The Flute Ship
Castricum

The
FLUTE SHIP
Castricum

Amy England

TP

TUPELO PRESS
Dorset, Vermont

Acknowledgments

Octopus and *Compass* have appeared in ACM.

Nothing Framed Is Accident has appeared in AMERICAN LETTERS AND COMMENTARY.

Waiting Table has appeared in CHICAGO REVIEW.

Can't See Fuji–Interesting and *One of the Dead Languages* have appeared in COLORADO REVIEW.

In a Suburb of Tokyo has appeared, and *Prologue, One Bought a Finch in a Wicker Cage And*, and *Everything Absent Gets Translated* will appear in CONNECTICUT REVIEW.

Endnotes, A Face's Three Chakras and *Surprised by Opera* have appeared in THE GERM.

We Have Been Waiting a Long Time has appeared in HIGH PLAINS LITERARY REVIEW.

For Ralph Mills and *Attic Shape* have appeared in INDIANA REVIEW.

At the Office, Abundant Coffee has appeared in INTERNATIONAL POETRY REVIEW under the title "Hermes' Mine."

For Elizabeth Ricketts has appeared in LIT.

What to Do with Inanimate Objects, Pale Cristóbal, and *Nothing Framed Is Absent* have appeared in NEW ORLEANS REVIEW.

Chrysopidae, Hermobiidae has appeared in NORTHWEST REVIEW.

The Still Wet Mud Tablets of the Law III has appeared in QUARTERLY WEST.

Calvados has appeared in SONORA REVIEW.

Afterword: Two Arts has appeared in TOUCHSTONE.

Two Tourists with Guide Book Approach Planetarium, What People and Crows Say, and *On the Beach* have appeared in TRIQUARTERLY.

Selections from *Seeing in My Sleep* will appear in VOLT.

Contents

For Mary Olson and Robert Uptain

DEDICATIONS

A Face's Three Chakras

(For Christine Hume)

Fear of reading in public has a cause and location.

Sometimes the black foam head of the microphone was over her mouth, obscuring its shapes, sometimes higher up, like a clown nose put on backwards. Mostly it was between her eyes, connecting them together.

Then the dwarves came up the trap door from their prison under the podium. You said words, broke the spell, hero, or rather, heroine, liberatrix, *vive l'improbable.* Carried her on their shoulders to another place entirely, had her read to them for years on end. She grew tired though it was flattering, her brows pulled together always.

Surprised by Opera

(For Catherine Kasper)

    All conventions of singing are silly, but only unfamiliar ones appear so. One night I rounded a blind corner just as a middle-aged couple bore down on me with their bicycles, just as the man began an aria from *Don Giovanni*. You will understand when I tell you that I was not
    prepared. This is about me, really. Never getting to finish my stories.

    Ma in Ispagna–remember how in the dark, under red lighthouse revolutions, the sound of his engine seemed more solid than the car? "Regrets, signori, signore," he said, or words to that effect, "you must take this raucous telescope elsewhere."

Hermes as a Victim of His Own Nature

(For Reginald Shepherd)

It was a late night; tires were hissing in the blue and red wet; people were grouped in certain ways; saxophone solos burst out, would not fit inside the clubs; lies were believed; a stack of old books was the prize in a card game.

Now you lie in the dark, wearing the robe your step-mother hates, its pattern of shut eyes. Usually you choose carefully what to read before sleep, but tonight you opened your winnings at random and happened on the words, "the all ensphered in the alchemist's egg." Your eyes won't close for delight, and under the bed, your shoes itch.

Pale Cristóbal

(For Jan Gorak)

You were staked to the campus lawn, spouting heresies. The fire caught on gasoline, then wood, but didn't hurt you in your asbestos skin. Your voice the center of the fire, like Yaweh, yelling, Christopher Ricks, Tell me–

You were staked to the campus, fire caught, blazed, center of fire, like Yaweh.

Staked. Campus. Center of fire. Salamander yelling Tell.

Things that Fall from the Sky Decoded

(For Rikki Ducornet)

In the almost full eclipse, the leaves pinholed crescent suns in hundreds on the street. The crescents looked like waves. The street looked underwater.

> *You will be persuaded by well-meaning friends to accompany them on a yacht outing. Under smiling weather and a little moon you will get sucked down by the water intake. The boat will later resurface, but none of you.*

The last ember of the fire sparked and waned in the wind: the halfway point between it and the orange brightest star on Scorpio's back was the peak of the tallest dead volcano in the ridge above us.

> *Neither you nor your animals will care in that fall of skin-dissolving blue crescents if the disaster was natural or caused by human agency.*

A spider in mid-air, its legs busy. A jet was plowing a white furrow towards it. Just as it arrived, a swift sailed through, making this a triple alignment. The important thing, however, was that all three bodies were the same size, as the Hundred Years' War is the same size as the cut on my leg.

> *You will end badly. You will all end very badly.*

The Fan

(for Kerry Minato)

I was two. My parents took me to the house where we were going to live. It was empty and I thought would continue so; the expectation of moving always through that white, unbroken space was delight. I was sitting on the floor laughing. My mother laughed, too, I assumed for the same reason.

The kitchen of my first apartment was a green cave unadulterated by furniture. Sometimes I sat on the floor of it and cried, but more and more I played music and danced around it. And sometimes voices came down through the fan over the stove–sounds of making love, then fights. I couldn't make out words. I can tell you this: by the time my solitude became easy, they had ceased to speak. There was a piano. I heard it in the afternoons, and pictured a sullen face over the passionate movement of hands.

For Elizabeth Ricketts

Pouring tea, I said to my visitor that it must be overwhelming to enter any possible strand of time at will. You'd think it would be unbearable, he answered, but actually, one traces out the lines one likes best, and tends to think of those as the most real. For example, no matter what universe I inhabit, I cannot help thinking of your doorman as the best orchestra conductor of North America, even though through most chains of cause and effect he never finishes his secondary education—(he sipped tea from my gold-rimmed cup, patterned with violets).

You must have wanted to see me in one of my less fortunate manifestations, I said. This is about as good as it gets, for you, he said. I pondered it. In my mean and empty apartment, the violet tea cup and the smell of Darjeeling were the only beautiful things.

Then you must like it here, in spite of the loss of the orchestra conductor, I said, or you would not bother to visit. Pleasure is not the only reason for travel, he said. And then: There is a catalpa tree growing just here, and as the orchid-like flowers drop, a string trio is playing Brahms. The violinist of this trio is the best woman in all the possible worlds, and I am hoping to find the time in which she will love me, or at least consent to speak to me for a few minutes. But that won't happen here, obviously. Although I always liked this cup. He left; I was never satisfied with the world again.

For Ralph Mills

Cottonwood, twig of. Note orange pith. And the leaf scar's shallow U shape, three veins. Buds reddish black, one missing, have some fragrance when crushed.

I took an umbrella out back to hook down a branch, broke off a piece. Set in a glass of water to instruct. What are catkins? Spikes, male or female, usually erect in this case drooping, typical of *Salix*: willow, cottonwood, poplar, aspen. The green flowers without petals will brown, grow, crack, shed seeds; the yard will be a box of down. Leaves yellow a few at once. An open tree, a hundred feet. As it matures, the grey bark furrows.

White aspens are grey rough at trunk, like wainscoting on a plaster wall, and deer walk through the room it makes, not here though. The soft yard. When he was a boy his father said Watch. Struck match, quick edge of fire and the white was gone.

Offering
(My Grandfather as Egyptian Bas-Relief)

Not gotten far, in these three months. Only to the vestibule, where a hawk watches the weighing of your soul. The feather. The pen it makes.

Dinner laid out, all gathered, drink giddiness. There are flute and drums playing from far off; the sun dies behind the pepper mill and chimneys. It's like always. But look aslant, there are pillars under earth, the hallway that begins your travels. Dead you are someone else–with those eyes become caves, you are dignified, a statue. Already nothing I say will make you turn and look at me.

Wine swallowed, meat, grain. For the good journey. The crocodile god won't devour you, nor forgetting drown you in its dark. And if you do sink into the living as into a pool and vanish there, at least with the quill pen death gives us, I will write it once: How clearly I see you.

Orchard

(With Apologies to Catherine Gresham)

Great Great Grandmother Anderson was still taking care of her grown son Milton Virgil, who was getting crazier all the time, and she thought that everything would be better if she bought this peach orchard in Kentucky. She moved down from Iowa and tended the peaches herself. Milton Virgil continued to get crazier until even living in a peach orchard wasn't enough, and he had to be sent to an institution. Great-Great Grandma, with tears in her eyes, put her boy on the train and charged the conductor to keep an eye on him. But the train derailed and Milton Virgil escaped and spent months running wild in the mountains, living God only knows how, until he was finally caught and popped into the sanitarium, where he very soon died.

The story I remember goes that way. But when I recently asked my great aunt to tell it again, it turned out that I had every particular wrong. It was not Milton (Milton Shakespeare: Grandmother Anderson was quite a reader), but *Clinton* Virgil who was a stark raving lunatic, and Grandmother Anderson longed to leave Iola, Illinois, to go to Arkansas, not Kentucky, because she had asthma (the connection is clear to no one). She got a cabin (which may or may not have had an incidental peach orchard attached) in the Ozark Mountains, and when she couldn't control Clinton Virgil any more, she had him institutionalized there. Only later, when she was trying to send Clinton down to stay with Milton Shakespeare in Mobile, did she put him on the train, and there was no accident, the conductor only didn't watch him like he'd promised, and Clinton got away. He did wander around for a very long time in the mountains before he got caught. Grandma Anderson, who now acted like she'd never had asthma in her life, didn't stop worrying about him for a second. (But you won't want to write about that, my aunt said. No one else in our family was ever crazy.)

Judy Spencer once told me about something that happened when she was doing a detasseling job. They were standing on the edge of the field, and of course at detasseling time the corn is eight or nine feet tall. A man walked out of the rows. He had a long, dirty beard, and he was wearing a woman's dress. He stared without seeming to see them, then turned around and walked back into the corn and disappeared. The country–there was no place to run aground once the corn was harvested, but no one ever saw him again. When I heard about Uncle Milton or Clinton escaping from the train and running wild, the first thing I thought was, "That's who I saw," forgetting that the two events were eighty years apart, that the Ozarks were nowhere near where I lived, that I was not actually present in either story.

Waiting Table

(For Lucy, Sarah, and Ben)

I

Love to you all. I haven't been home
in a long time.
I have good news. After looking for
months, I finally found work

At Nirvana. It's good work. I have many duties.

II

With an ocher plastic ewer I water
The green vines of Nirvana,
Water the dining ones and dance their ice.

A touched button unspools
A nasal, tricky music. I align
The table clothes' four corners,
Gather crumbs up from the rich

Patterned rugs. Nirvana must be clean.

In November with a yellow broom
I sweep the brick portal free of leaves.

III

What can I tell you? Life continues to be decorative rather
than structured—handling fantastic stuffs, cash in large amounts and distance,
cassette tapes of weird drums. I touch struck lucifers to spice bush wands, and
waft by, trailing threads of smoke, more Art Nouveau than Mucha's Bernhardt

I can show you the votive candles.
The tables' fluted glass spheres house them and become
Lucidas floating clear among the brass and salt.
Their twin lights swim up clear again from the depths of Lucite table tops.

And the lumen hours accumulate
Like gold beads on a bracelet
Not overly opulent. I keep my hours short.
To love a place forever, don't spend too much

Time there.

IV

I've been bussing tables, been jamming pickled chilies into little metal cups lest they eat through the plates. I've been making my hands permanently greasy unwrapping chicken parts, which by the way I've come to loathe.

And taking squares of cloth
And tucking up stainless
In ritual folds,
Or random folds if busy–

And bringing out at decorous intervals
Trays of food and spice
In their myriad combinations
For hands to hover over, choose from.

V

If you wonder about the place all these things point to, the wall hangings repeatedly depict it. Nirvana, I can tell you, has obscenely rounded hills, blue skinned princes on jeweled elephants, no sense of perspective, women in light saris, their revealed breasts dripping ivory beads like milk. Everyone walks in step there, and in the same direction. Eyes are like hieroglyphs; few right hands are empty of symbols. And leaves of some laurel-like plant border everything.

VI

This basement room, dim and pink
As the interior of a shell,
This is spice church. Bow to the far,
Fork in hand, bow and eat

That country of elephant jewelry.
Take it in and swallow it. Converse. Say,
"When I go to India," or for more effect, "The week
I was in India..."
                    The inner sanctum in chaos. Spice on the floor, ice on the
floor, towers of dishwashings, smears of spilled lassi. The boss argues and
cooks at the end of the phone cord,

Opaque monosyllables.
Her few free moments given over
To the pages of *The Case*
Of the Three-Legged Heiress, she eats standing.

VII

The table's final gold is no fire, no
Description of color. Bright leavings
Of lucre wafers, signifying departure, signifying

Change.

Once the money's enough, I'm off, Roma, Britain, Lucerne, Bengal, the light-piked Israeli walls, Sahara's great nothing. Tourism is true worship. I won't be my boss, for instance–poor thing, poor sad mistake, to really reach your place of distance. To love a place forever–

It's long since I've been home, and will be long. I love you.

VIII

While I am not home,

My overcoat, my pike, my painted trillium,
My light and lady and favored son and givers of all affection,
Sarai, Benoni, Luke,

This lucubration must serve, benami,
To conjugate the one act: *amo, amas,*
Amamus, amatis–Sarabaites, loose leaves, leave
Soon, and gather

strange things to tell me, years from now, when we meet. More than anything, I love

Stories of travel.

CYPANGU

/20

Prologue

Sitting at the end of a room, looking down.
Look up, eyes' white corners'
electric flash. And when you talked, you were language's
favorite, sharing private jokes like
some high school clique I wanted into.

Inadequate. I want to shake you sometimes–
You know so much, tell me what to say to

make you stay in the frame.
But years, the room stretch long;
You vanish to a flyspeck,

Mnemosyne pill, swallowed away.
At least will well armed children come
knocking to be let out

in sentences in spears that hit
what they aim for…

In a Suburb of Tokyo

I

Rustling over the river
could be bats, too dark to say.

And for stars, only
the green and gold cat stares
sometimes appear, a sort of stars,
then slip off, and their shadows
brush messages on walls,
the maze of streets.

II

Can't see, say what I see,
not even child's alphabet inventory of
cat fish star

Hearing from the bridge
splashes in the cement bed
of the River of Many Geese,
where invisible bright orange and white and orange

carp sleep with open eyes

At the Office, Abundant Coffee

Crammed maze of desks, whole floor of a small building, typewriters'
syncopated clock tick, flash the color of absinthe, spitting copies. Salesmen
on telephones adding jazz ornaments of improvised information. Smell of burnt
coffee and liquid paper. Three or four backs crouched in interview, assess,
assess. What is your name? Where do you live? Occasional mild earthquakes
are the bass.

Cup after miniature paper cup of weak burnt coffee.
What is your name. *Yes.* No, what is–
If they write 3, that means: Although your grammar skills are well developed,
Write 7, it means: you still require some conversation practice to become fluent.

Do teachers' reports. Read: Students liked free conv. Type:
The students enjoyed free conversation, and given the hands-on nature of the course, we
spent a large portion of each session discussing relevant topics.
Great class. Lot of fun. Type:
The fervor of this class for the acquisition of language was the single most inspiring
experience in my entire career as an educator.
Coffee. This is not

A yes or no question. What is your *job*. Oh. I am
Quality control manager. What—

The shaft to Hermes' mine may as well start
from the office of Tokyo English Institute

as anywhere. Answers like ore hacked fresh
from the mother lode–they smell like burnt coffee,
and they don't look silver, are neither crafted nor quick.
Even after refining, you can hardly tell them
from the rock, the random noise
where they were born. I confess, my lust
for the metal of sense has dulled
from handling it in such heaps such new dirt What
What is
What is your name I do not
Understand

Compass

Say only what is there

Against a sky innocent of color
Over cream gold buildings and blue grey steel
Fire escapes and railings, next to a red
Neon sign whose color could be blood
If this were about blood

Roofcrow rawks, spreads
Its old umbrella limbs, flaps off
Wing feathers splayed like talons
Rake air, a violence

This is not about violence
This is about a bird shaped hole was riven
Through the sky forever
But that hole moved and spoke
As if it lived
Crow black crow
Your mind's a bright

Needle; you know where you are going.

Questions of Beauty,   Questions of Place

Flowers were   answers,   men sometimes   questions;
that one there   who loves   nonchalance   would probably hate his
lady–slipper made   of beads. Some flowers weren't luminous; some were bad for you:
the photographer's   decadent   Indian pipe,   glowing yellow-
green like neon   on   the dark   ground.
Another was   a sun   incomparably   blue in a
white sky,   smudged as a grade school pastel,   wouldn't be looked at closely,
as we all rode to the beautiful
                     place.   Scrambling   up a wooded
ridge outside of Enoshima,   night   coming couldn't
find   the train   station.   Avalanche
of loose earth   bark mold   earth worms   and I look
up from my   hands   gripping saplings into the face of a freckled white
lily alone   on its stem.
Life is gold leaf   wearing   thin on a black   lacquer box.
This is not home, why do I   intrude myself,   and the lily turned to me
its kiln-lit   interior

What People and Crows Say

Eight people in red robes, crows land and rise, won't settle. All by a pond, a poor round puddle ringed with mud. The eight drop a hundred kinds of seeds, not for the crows, but the crows eat them completely. Veils cover the people's eyes to protect them from visions, so the birds are only rustling and hoarse remarks.

The way one doesn't notice sounds until they're pointed out. "That crow" Robert was very angry "has been making a nuisance of itself for two straight days. What does it want?" And nothing could be more demanding than that constant rasp, which now I have no choice but to hear.

The painting was made for an evil purpose. A girl bought it at a flea market. She steps back, then up to straighten it. Does her pleasure cancel out the sentence that the artist said at the picture's completion? "Such red," she thinks, "those blurs of wings."

For no reason, our cat cries and cries. *"O-Karasu-sama,"* I say, "little black one, Princess Crow." When addressed she is quiet; her tail's end twitches.

The seeds are eaten. Dusk, and a crow lands on a branch. He shakes darkness from his wings like dust from a carpet—he is to evening what the rooster is to sun-up. Calls, strident and restless, but he can't really be discontent, as the world becomes like himself.

Rainy Season

Rust mites have eaten it
Down to a half-life
Lace of corrosion.

Three posts,
Three crossbars. Some bats flap over

The grey everything,
But this red is not digestible,
Can see every pockmark and Swiss cheese hole.

Six rectangles
In Urayasu without lines.

There are ten feet of railing
Alone on the walls of Edo River,

Like a fish hook stuck rusting
In the maw of grey everything.
Some gulls glide by.

We have climbed the wall and sit, discussing
The railing, its heroic qualities.

Hand scraped, sweaty lines
Stained with rust. Don't remember touching it–
Must have done.

Like the railing abraded
Into identity.

Like mouth stinging with
Kisses that didn't
Hurt at the time.

Nothing Framed Is Accident

Temple: a rope
pulled taut between stakes whose number
is *shi,* death. Square to frame chance
flying birds, auguries.

In the frame of a foreign temple, your arms
iron at my back, your mouth

made my mouth. It's this
shock of supple, surprise tendons
I want words to say.

I wanted words
to be your body, but it became
flying birds; seven wingbeats
pulsed through it.

Seven are the cries
I once committed to air–
Seven swans I follow across nations,
trying to knit with words the nettle shirts

that make them human.

Nothing Framed Is Absent

Floating isle, Cypangu:
retreating behind Atlantic, Pacific
as voyage widens the world.

Noble island…fertile in pearls,
shrine and residence walled with gold.
Error reveals it, that crevice

the birds love. See how thick
they roost under the worm–eaten eaves
carved with clouds.

How the world's corners are marked
with monuments. Here an iron bell
blackly garners the year's
hundred and eight mistaken wants.

Here the priest's family's
housed. They've shucked off
bicycles and shoes at the door, and rest now
to rain ticking down
chains of iron flowers.

In the miniature necropolis, flowers have been offered
to the doll-like dead
named on flat sticks
rain erases
I'd rather be a name washed from a stick
than forgo you, Beautiful Mistake.

Fourth corner: from serrate elm the lamplight
spotted us like leopards; our arms, sides were
strange and quick.
Gold gleamed behind shutters where
the Buddha kept awake among dead
chrysanthemums; white koy ghosted the black pond.

You told so few of your thoughts; I've had to guess at
that retreating island of wit and leopards running
fleet in vapor over snow. And the walled
gold towns.

One Bought a Finch in a Wicker Cage And

Between dark and dark,
miraculous birds flash through five red pillars,
and I lean against the pillar of listen.

Your voice a touch to be leaned into,
utterance hanging like smoke in air,
head bending down–

tobacco has changed your tongue
to a cat's rasp, and I step
into the peat
ghost behind swallowed whiskey.

Everything Absent Gets Translated

In the purifying salt, what appears,
vanishes: rain smoke iron gold
vanished birds, you're not here
to hear their translation,

and so the unslaked temple must be
carried continually, the miracle in it
rattling, finger bone
in a reliquary box.
Unbearable music, it decorates
the plod of step that transports it.

Why do we call these lacks gold, why make graves
wanton with flowers? To complicate
the casket, its edges–
the eye needs to take long
finding its way.
Error once ridden into grace, there's nothing else.

Only we can't
leave off translating (With my body,
I thee worship)–partial, treacherous–

"Can't See Fuji/—Interesting"

Open door
Frame for our
Done labor:

Downrush of slope, slither of dark
Brown scree (whispering
Vesicular basalt), and up
Lumbering cut, path marked with white

Cast down trash. We sat on the floor
Of the seventh station, eating dinner,
And watched the open square

Plaster over
With iris blue
Fog of absolute
Opacity

Work dimmed away, way
Undone. It was late, and we had just
Escaped erasure.

Bite and then bite
Of steam and rice in the
Warmed throat, eyes fixed
As if on the movie's most

Exciting moment,
Ice or iris wall
Of arriving night.

One of the Dead Languages

Streets empty and echoing; I read aloud:

> *Love, a wind*
> *Blowing the tree's branches*
> *All one way.*

Those dead authors, I said.

> *Hands, feet must guide themselves.*
> *I won't leave off thinking of you.*

Imagine

being able to write that.

> *What was I doing I was*
> *Bowsprit leaning into*
> *Wind, love, froth of waves at my breast.*

And now you are a continent,

> *An ocean away.*
> *Still I think any turned corner*
> *Will show you to me.*

I'm sending on this dreadful book, lacking irony;

> *I let my thoughts travel*
> *The wrinkling ocean, the night span*
> *Of America, to imagine your sleep;*

my throat aches reading it.

You are a town at rest, and I
Run in the uplands, and howl under the moon.

Afterword: Two Arts

"Franz Kline, oil on cardboard." Black swirl, and the oil afterglow is pleasure. Before starting a painting he did many preparatory studies.

the making stroke   caressive

Flicking a bit of white thread off a black shoulder.

Do you remember that hour we were waiting to climb the mountain? That park? There was a boys' ping-pong team. Some had paddles, most did not, swinging practice strokes in time together empty handed.

Pretend to sign a name in air, a flourish, study the neon motion you have made.

Here's another picture of our trip. The team was running laps; an arrangement occurred. I'd climbed a tree, looked down through a gap in the tufts of needles to the white path. Like tossed jacks, seven or eight heads of sleek, sealy black, elbows and feet showing and vanishing:

editive   strike shut

Pleasure in this case preceded. I saw the photograph approach, snapped the shutter.

Like calligraphy, but also a railway bridge seen from below against a white sky, as if that industrial ruin had just happened, scrawled writing, pick-up-sticks.

"What's the character for *fude*?" I asked a woman on the train. With her finger, she traced the strokes on her palm. "Like so," she said, showing the palm to me.

Not a photograph: Your hand pulled my hand; we lay under the strong presence of stars. The galaxy was bearing down, a circular saw
       cutting dark metal with its
       centrifugal spin:

            editive   the making stroke

      Light undoes what dark creates.
We toiled up the night mountain,
       flew down the day.

Word nor ground. Not engraved or grave (or heart dark under hand). The claim I have on you is in
       the playing language. Empty hands. Lightsome: Listen to what I'm going to say.

Endnotes

The barbarian heart is hard to fathom; the Throne ponders
And dares not relax its armed defense...
Do we not bear ox knives to kill but a chicken,
Trade our most lovely jewels for thorns?

                    –Rai Sanyoo

To "The Birth of the Land"

Complete and solidify this drifting land! This commanded the heavenly deities.

Izanagi and Izanami: He-who-invites and She-who-invites

Floating Heavenly Bridge: The six quarters are east west, north south, above below.

They held counsel together: When I met Reiko the first time, the cafeteria around us immediately became ugly. America, illuminated by her exile, was shabby, used, cheap,

saying, Is there not a country beneath? Cf. Coen, "In the observed latitude of 24 deg. 6 minu. saw, shortly after the noon, a large band of foam, mixed with a turbulence of current, wherein we saw many Portuguese Man-of-War and rock-weed, and round jelly-fishes and a piece of wood; which might be sure signs of land; but could see no land."

Thereupon they thrust down the Jewel Spear of Heaven, and groping about therewith: As the plane descended there were gaps in the clouds, through which a crabbed, various scenery, the brief mirror gleam of drowned fields

found the ocean. A man. Looking out at Nagasaki Bay from the balcony of his study.

They stirred the salt water koworo-koworo "In the Morning at dawning it began to blow stiffly from the S.S.E., so that the sea within a short time became violently hollow, caused by the current which runs against the wind, and the sea which beats against the grounds; and a dense mist set also in...It is here everywhere high land, what is to be seen in the draught

And the brine from the spear coagulated and became an island which received the name of Ono-goro-jima you find a low-lying bight, bearing North, and the high sand-dune, appearing like Kyckduyn at Huysduynen. This point we gave the name of Santduynige Hoeck, and is from the witte gepleckte hoeck, N.E. by N. about 12 leagues."

The two deities thereupon descended and dwelt in this island (easier said). A man sitting in a winter house on the mud fan of Deshima. Four years in coming to Japan, he is now twenty paces from it, but cannot get there.

Accordingly they wished to become husband and wife together, and to produce countries. Accordingly I became a professional alien in a small trading company, staring out windows, pretending to compose a business letter.

...made Ono-goro-jima the center of the pillar of the land. I, on the other hand, can't see any land.

Then the male deity inquired of the female deity, In thy body, is there aught formed? Thunberg faithfully followed the theories of Linnaeus, who insisted that the generative organs were the key to classifying plants,

She replied, saying, My body, formed though it be formed, comparing calyx to labia minora, corolla to labia majora,

has one place which is formed insufficiently. Earth the plant's belly, *vasa chylifera* the roots, bones stem, lungs leaves, heart heat

Then Izanagi said, my body...has one place...which is formed to excess. There are sheets of pressed flowers on Thunberg's table. *Aster dubius. Amethystea caerulea. Verbena officialis,* common vervain, Juno's tears. It grows everywhere. He writes:

Therefore, I would like to take that place in which my body is formed to excess and insert it into that place in thy body which is formed insufficiently, and thus give birth to the land. How would that be? "I therefore earnestly desire you to permit me to sojourn on the mainland a sufficient time to accomplish my research, to our two countries' mutual benefit."

Now the male deity turning by the left, and the female by the right, Reiko, whose name means the sound of jewels, ultimate debutante, idea of east, married her gardener lover,

they went round the pillar of the land separately and nothing as interesting has happened to her since, to her relief. The world has narrowed to home again, and caught me in its pinch.

When they met together on the other side, the female deity spoke first: In the case of *Salvia japonica,* the two stamens within the bilabiate corolla meet late in anthesis,

Ana-ni-yasi, I have met with a comely youth! touching their anthers to the forked pistil, and then curl back around the inflexed outer lobes of the lower lip.

Izanagi was displeased: How is it that thou, a woman, shouldst have been the first to speak? "I hope you will not think me unmindful of your profound hospitality in this request...Your obedient servant, Carl Thunberg, physician to the Jan Compangie embassay."

Nevertheless, they commenced to live as husband and wife. Rei, whose name is an arrow from a point, idea of east, doubtful star.

And gave birth to LEECH-CHILD, who even at the age of three could not stand upright. "At the time 3 glasses of the second watch had passed, saw still the light of our consort, but lost sight of it soon."

Accordingly, they gave birth to the ROCK-CAMPHOR-REED-BOAT-OF-HEAVEN, in which they placed the leech child, and abandoned it to the winds. "With God's help, we got clear of the land. Looking around for our consort [that is, the flute ship *Castricum*], but could nowhere see her, over which we were sad again, did not know what to think whether she was lost or not."

Nor did their minds take pleasure in the next birth, which was of the island Ahaji. "The island which will not meet," i.e., is not satisfactory. May also be interpreted as "my shame." The characters with which this name is written mean "foam road." Perhaps the true derivation is "millet-land."

To "Princess Yamato and Prince Plenty"

After this Yamato-toto-hi-momo-so-bime no Mikoto (Princess Japan; 日 *ni,* sun, + 本 *hon,* origin; Idea, that is, of East)

became the wife of Onamochi (also O-mono-nushi, the Great Land-lord God). I work on the tenth floor, in Nihonbashi, not far from that hotel where the Dutch ambassador stayed each year to greet the emperor. The physician was always a great draw, and a hundred scholars of Edo came to question him.

This god, however, was never seen in the daytime. What is unfamiliar one sees utterly, with the staring of an infant (feel the eyes go round and blue),

but then how do I know what I have seen? *"As my Lord comes only at night, I am unable to view his august countenance distinctly."* I must study the map all over again. That night is North is old age, winter water, black tortoise. South, the noon where I am now, is phoenix fire, red of weddings.

The spring that Thunberg waited for is a topiary dragon, East, childhood, blue (for *blue* read *green*). *"I beseech him therefore to delay a while:"* The year seems to have stopped at June. Each day the hot concrete drives me in and up, to office to apartment, to any removal no matter how unsatisfactory. *"That I may look upon the majesty of his beauty."* The Great God answered and said,

"Tomorrow I will enter thy toilet case and stay there." Tomorrow, I will enter thy toilet case and stay there.

"I pray thee be not alarmed at my form" which opens to the eye like fire flowers, boom, red, bloom, white…I want the Eden of knowing a thing for the first time, over and over, without end.

Princess East wondered secretly in her heart at this. In the morning windows, all that is ungrounded floats by, a green balloon, a black plastic bag upright as if carried. *Waiting until daybreak, she looked.* A sheet of blank paper spirals up and out of sight, never reaching the end of its updraft.

There was a beautiful little snake, here a bird, *Pterodroma leucoptera,* there a vine, *Bryonia japonica, of the length and thickness of the cord of a garment.* The lungs leaves. The bight like Kyckduyn. This isn't like anything.

Thereupon she was frightened, and uttered an exclamation–

The Great God…"Thou didst not contain thyself, but has caused me shame:" Night will come pressing, shouldering aside the blue and possible: *"I will in my turn put thee to shame."* Will stand in the window, lighted body exposed to the blank dark–

So treading the Great Void: The window washer spiders past, *so treading,* feet flat against the glass, *Great Void,*

he ascended to Mount Mimoro. I have a fine view from here of lost possessions on the rooftops, a sodden open Bible, a red plastic shoe. Objects should all be birds the way, muscular and rustling, they have eluded hands.

She looked up and disappeared into the tapestry of trees. I can hear *and had remorse* the bird-flute of her crying.

Throws herself on the bed, the tears, why did you marry me, when I had thought her dignity would bear anything. *She flopped down on a seat and with a chopstick stabbed herself in the pudenda so that she died.* Hygrophilia lancea: intimacy, that spear. *She was buried at O-chi.*

Men called that place the Chopstick Tomb. Thunberg examines the flattened stems of the *Erigeron* (man early old) which he has *men* called *scadens,* creeping. An interpreter gave it in exchange for a diagram of the chambers of the heart heat phoenix *tomb.*

It was made by men in the daytime, and by the gods at night. Death is a metal, a tiger, West, an autumn slow in coming. It is built of white *stones carried from Mount O-saka.* Meanwhile, I'm pleading with the houses, streets, the very stones, *gods at night,* don't reveal yourselves yet to me.

Now the people standing close to each other "sculler-boat came along-side, was manned with 7 scullers and 5 nothing-doing Japanese; brought us 4 fine red rock-breams aboard, for which *standing close* we gave them some rice." *Passed the stones from hand to hand* and if I had a stone in hand, I'd command it to be a geode that wouldn't break, a gem no one would trade for.

And thus transported them To spear and fix the living object. I wish, Reiko, I could unlearn your name. To the funeral bell, *Salvia,* Thunberg added the clapper *japonica*: from the mountain to the tomb. "The water was here very foul and green." A man need not fear death who has sage in his garden.

SEEING IN
MY SLEEP

Seeing in My Sleep

At the beach, I run into my friend Bela, with her doll-like hands and heavy accent. She is dyeing the sand with colored powders to prepare for a birthday party. Already the beach is a spectrum of a hundred shades. The cake, large enough to jump out of, sits on the sand right where the waves come up, but it's so big that it won't matter if the bottom gets wet. Bela: "I wish I could talk. So busy." I don't mind that I'm not invited to stay. As I climb up the dunes, the evening is growing blue, and guests are beginning to arrive, masked in white and silver, trailing chimes of small bells, dressed like Pegasus, Pierrot, the moon.

A candy store–the Lucite bins are full of jellybeans. Some are round, some rectangular, and their flavors are labeled. Lilac, peridot, opal, iris, hematite. The garnet ones look like pomegranate seeds and taste faintly sweet, but so cold they hurt the teeth.

Up in Lucy and Sarah's bedroom there is a salamander trying to run up the wall of the closet. Brown with pale eye spots, like a hagfish has, and you can hear it scratching. Mother says, "Its legs are making orange circles in the air." I try to put a paper bag over it, but it runs, tail flicking up the inside of my ankle, cold, wet and foul.

There's a python in the kitchen making me nervous. I don't feel up to catching it, so I turn on the gas, go into the next room, carefully closing the door behind me. Thumps, crashing, death throes–I know that huge loops of snake, thick as a tree, are arching frantically around the kitchen. Its head isn't visible, nor the end of its tail.

I think, "What if Joe decides to use the back door? He'll come to harm," but even though it's quiet now, I can't bring myself to check the kitchen just yet. All comes out well however. Joe eels in through the little bedroom window. I say, "What, again no clothes?" Not so; he points to his single piratical earring.

Later, in the kitchen, I gather pieces of dead snake into a burlap bag.

Brandeis University looks like an English countryside. Maple leaves have aggregated into a large butterfly that flops past, green orange and on the edges brown, too clumsy to see in detail. All around it is green and cloudy. Two boys run up with a butterfly net. "Don't kill it," I say after them, following them in and out of low brick stables, dairy barns. It starts to rain. Struck by water, the leaves come apart and drift down; this strange life is over.

World War Three is coming; all Americans have to leave Tokyo. We crowd onto the underwater train. Bruce settles in next to me; I have the window seat. As the ocean floor streams by, we can see picnic tables and hibachis. The brown grass of what used to be a park is waving in the currents. Far off on the horizon, cigar shapes slant towards the bottom. They must be the size of dirigibles, but we realize they're fish.

Walking down an echoing dark hall to a business meeting. I look over–my husband has turned into a German shepherd, as he often does when he's not feeling sociable. His eyes are the same blue as before, and his white fur is tipped with black. Noses my hand, trots off, plume tail, nails clicking on the linoleum, knowing no one will mind him leaving now. We pretend to other people that he can't control it, you see. Handsome dog.

World War III has come and gone. Very fortunately, all of my friends have survived. Steve is there, thumping around in his cast, many others. We live together in a still intact, Frank Lloyd Wright-ish sort of A-frame house. Actually, it was built by scientists to turn into a space ship, but no scientists are left to use it. And why should we leave? Life is good. Always cloudy now but it never rains, and everything we can fish out of the city's down-sifting dust is ours to keep. Evenings, we stagger back under the weight of the day's loot.

Then the real catastrophe comes, an earthquake, a comet approaching, something, and we have to take off in the house. Dark sky, deep rumbling, people whose existence we never suspected running out of the collapsing buildings and toward the river. We have enough room to save a few, and only minutes to decide which ones. To a boy and girl climbing into a rowboat, I say imperiously, "Come with me."

No, don't go in that house. The devil lives in it, people do rituals. You wholesome-looking adolescents, out of some fifties movie, carrying your instrument cases, get off that porch. It's night, are you crazy? Satan's face is all pointy smiling, he knows you're coming. Your parents will never find you. They think you're at orchestra practice. A mote of consciousness, like a mosquito, I buzz around your silly hairdos; sometimes I pop into your heads to see what's there. Appalling ignorance. You have no idea, do you?

Well, the door's locked, so that's that, go home, but now someone's found a manhole cover and he's hauling it up. An iron ladder made of connected pentagrams descends endlessly under the house. Something about engineering, something about the cello—you exchange determined looks, nod, and start down.

The Duke and Duchess have decided on an ocean liner voyage. Ah, *la belle epoque*…for the baby, they have engaged a new wet nurse; I am with her now. She undoes the first few buttons on her dress–she wants to look ready for work, but not to have her bosoms spilling out all over. I believe the baby might be with the maid in the sauna. It's the next deck down, no, another, another. Here's the laundry room. Why do I keep noticing people's desiccated, curled up feet sticking out of corners? Here's the sauna, the swimming pool. A lot of steam, why is the light red, where's the baby, what is floating in the water?

After the apocalypse, we are all, under the enemy's control. A few of us still resist. We hide large automatic weapons in our army fatigues, then go into a store that sells sewing notions. They look like the sewing notions of a century ago because the world has really regressed. Secretly I write a coded message on the inside of a designated spool of thread.

Several generations after the apocalypse, completely in the enemy's control. No one goes outside who can afford to stay in; not many men are left. When girls reach eleven or twelve, their fathers marry them off to their friends and allies.

A girl with black hair is standing at the window of her bedroom in what used to be a Hilton Hotel, now the house of her numerous family. She is looking out on the Sahara which covers the world. It's her wedding night, but she has only the dimmest picture of what that means.

No stars now, it's always cloudy. An iron framework has been built out on the sand with tiny lights attached to it, made to look like stars. She doesn't know how unconvincing it is. Two of the kitchen boys are playing on the frame like a jungle gym. She knows why they're playing there even though she's never left the house, never imagined leaving. One hangs by his knees. Both are laughing in the poisonous air.

A row of empty houses growing shabbier and more ornate as the afternoon dies away. Passing a mass of gingerbread and cobwebs, a house like Miss Havisham's wedding cake, a Japanese family in traditional dress trudges out their exile. The husband is abusive–the wife's debt to him is enormous, unpayable. She wearily ignores him, as does their son.

Then I run up as a young man, a *ronin* whose heart has been touched by the woman's sorrow, sword waving and shouting at the husband, "You're not wanted here. The marriage debt is a dead custom, and so will you be if you don't leave." He snarls as he runs off.

Now the evening light is red, and the three of us lie on the ground; the narration says, "And everyone there wanted to be there, and all of the bodies were real bodies." This means that 1) this is a true family who chose to be a family, unlike the old demon of a father, or that 2) the bodies are corpses; the father has come back and killed them all, as they all secretly wished.

They're coming. Windows and doors. I shut and shut. Pulling down bars, turning locks. I forgot the next room. I forgot the second floor. Pressing my hand along sashes trying to force down misshapen frames. The back door. As I reach it, a man in an army uniform is there, crouched next to the laundry basket, turning to see me. Woodenness spreads up from the floor through my legs.

My bedroom, like a watch tower, has windows on all sides. Before the sun comes up, the yard is intensely blue and green. My love, hair curled like a Greek statue's, waiting for me to come down and run away with him. The back stairs, quietly the back door, swift and soft. He's so sad. His father just died. He's sinking into the ground; now only his head remains. I kneel down and say comforting things until he's whole in my arms, but his mind's a black tunnel. Snowflakes, size of quarters, silver of quarters, light only on us, intricate in our hair, evaporate. "Your father sent them for his blessing," I tell him. So, he says, so what, it doesn't change anything. His mind's a black tunnel. I look up and the window's an angel, with blue light streaming from her red wings, oh, look…I think, so? Nothing's any different. And then I realize who this man is.

Sarah is a red granite angel lying down in a place the tribe leaves alone. In the millennia since the apocalypse, the new dark ages built a cathedral there. Later the new age of factories made a cheap diner out of it. Now the courtyard is cracked with weeds, and the disparate sections of architecture are equally meaningless to us. We let the ghosts have it.

I discover I can fly, not high up, but skimming the ground fast, if I don't lose concentration. So I'm not afraid of ghosts any more, and hum out to the old place to retrieve Sarah from the statue. I'll grab her hand, I'm thinking, and she'll be pulled out of the stone. As long as we're holding hands, she'll be able to float too. Every time my attention wavers, I dip down; my feet hit stones and roots.

CHICAGO
AS GALLERY
OF ICONS

/56

We Have Been Waiting a Long Time

The rails empty to their very
    meeting–Come Lantern-Eyed,
      anvil vector pounding on hot
blue stars…

    and wail past us unworthy ones,
      slapped with the wake of it,
        the guitar player's fingers working
silently, his open mouth while you scream.

Dictated by a Fellow Passenger on the Jeffrey Express

Thank you for riding the ChiCAgo TRANsit Authority.
We want you to have a VERY pleasant holiday, so please
Make sure ALL your personal belongings are...are in...are in the place
Where you keep your personal belongings.
Michigan Avenue. The final destination. Congress. Congress Hotel.

Keep your personal magnetism ON.
Say NO to deception, seduction, witchcraft. Study these things.
Learn to be alone, but not lonely. Say NO
To deception, for this is the season of deception.
Say No to seduction, No to adultery.
If I belong to one woman, why should I let
Another woman seduce me?
You with no desire have taken the first step
Towards a heavenly condition.
May the sun rise on your tomorrow. May the moon

Beam on your tonight.
May the spirit of the ancient artists protect you from seduction.
May the spirit of the Russian artist protect you.
May your heart beat 68 times per minute, and your blood pressure be 78/60.
May the bottoms of your feet be of positive podiatry
According to the temperature of the earth.
May your temperature be 98.6. May you never believe a lie.
Michigan. Adams. Art Institute. The secret.
The secret of the lions.

/58

Evanston or Maybe Highland Park

You must take my word on this. Summer of canvassing, and no matter how noble my cause I felt hangdog guilty and a nuisance and people saw it and gave me almost nothing. The friendlier their lawn ornaments, Hello! and the waving gnomes, the wreaths on the front doors, WELCOME FRIEND, WELCOME TO OUR HOME, the farther away they wished me for interrupting their dinner, for making them go through the work of deciding if I was legitimate or not, for reminding them once more that we don't really care about things that haven't yet effected us personally, often not even then.

The day was long, but the actual canvassing not so much–started at about four and ended at eight thirty or nine. Mostly what filled these hours was dread. The stretches between having been rejected and facing the next rejection were very brief. But there were a few moments, in some green place of privilege where the walk between houses was long enough to constitute its own event, when the sunlight was horizontal and yellow and the grass was luminous and the air was full of white, drift of cottonwood, upflung drops of sprinkler water, shouts of children, paired cabbage butterflies, when peace consumed me.

I simply could not always keep my guard up against the illusion of that place, that this self-contained green extended infinitely out to a world of old homes floating in flower beds and bridal wreath bushes, that refinishing furniture and lawn care and sports I disliked were sufficient topics of conversation. That the whole world was like my childhood, and that my childhood had been very different than it actually was. Wealth, limitless and dependable, water spouting up as from the fountains of Versailles, the trees and dandelions abundantly reseeding themselves on the accommodating air.

What I would like you to accept, what I wish we could agree on, was that these moments were not merely triumphs of nostalgia, nor breakdowns in the process of critical questioning (what did they do to earn all this, anyway⸮), that when I momentarily forget that the socio-economic basis of all of these full growth cottonwoods had its questionable aspects, what I was truly doing was... was...never mind...

Monroe Street Harbor

Within the almost meeting arms
Of break walls, what is embraced–
Red docking posts, yellow buoys,
A few furled boats shaped to knife the water,
Lovingly, randomly named, like race horses–
Jolly Roger, Poetaster, Joie de Vivre.

A grey shack stands on the dock amid bins
Labeled in prophecy ice, ice, ice.
Lighthouse light swings by, beats red, this might
Be the navel of everything. Masts
Swing and tongue
Bells of atmosphere
Over Michigan's liquid tick…

Summoning continually
To benches whose splinty planks
Bite legs and the chill ends of fingers, to sit
Among trees upholding
Canopies of arthritic complaint.

All given movement by rocking water, rising gulls,
Banners sounding off like cannons in the violent air.
All decked with the festive waste of fallen apples
Red globes and brown coins, perfumed
With the wine of that decay, and nothing can restrain
The profusion of things spilling out the cornucopia of *this day*.

Summoned as if to watch at the harbor theater
Some spectacle, some race
Of flowers to rotting fruit,
The year running toward its end in ice.
What is harbored is
A framed
Haven of forms, particularity, a kind of history.

Chrysopidae, Hermobiidae

I

I must admit it was satisfying–
The iridescence in the fold of the net,
Damselfly fanning out its last, the neat
Cemetery of pins.

I did at times feel crueler for it.
In the weakened killing jar, larger mantises
Lasted out hours, swiveling their tricorn heads
Above their G clef bodies to watch whatever moved.

And there was a walking stick
Skewered before its time.
It came to, paced the air, tried
To bend free its unbendable body.

But with the semester ending, order won out,
Order and making the count. A breathless push
With the pinning block, and the crane fly was in place,
Rigor mortis making visible its big blur of legs.

And the lacewings–salvation.
On the last night for the collection, I found dozens
In all their species, trying to marry the porch lamp.
They filled the empty spaces, their netty wings all

Small branched, oval, small, gold and green.
Their bodies were thumbnail slips,
Their red eyes, jewels.
They were exquisite. They were what I needed.

II

In winter, frost
Empties the window of views.
It suits that luminous white boredom to browse through
Boxes of pinned things…

All there, teeming mess
Of swarm and flit and scuttle
Made Latinate and still.
I brought their winter early.

I was that season, the little ends I made.

Octopus

Under streetlight:
      Rims of lit edge, his left side;
Right dark.

Eight strides off, already he's folded
      Into the curve of street,
All dark there like any want.

O pivot o head turned
      To look at something he wants far
More than you you

Motion or arc,

Pebble tossed
      Down the well–he's walking away–
And the small slap on water never sounds.

Or else it's all water sound,
      He's stone, you insatiable
Wave

Unbraiding yourself again
      On that fixity that cliff,
Back turned to you.

Has reach finally pulled you
      Out of your shape, metamorphosis,
Body to act, embodied act?

Monster with one desire, stretch long
      Your many arms;
He might come back.

Calvados

For George Olson

"Madam,"
said the snake,
taking a seat next
to me, "I'm glad you
also appreciate this rare
view. I find I require these
occasional rests during my walks"
–bowing–"lacking as I do your youth
and vitality." His hand was on his cane,
the ends of his goatee, his moustache, were
perfect points, and the gallantry! He bent down
his head to hear my questions. Yes, he had trouble
with his leg, a fall he'd suffered. The monocle because
his eyesight was not what it had once been. He wore a
white silk scarf–"I feel the cold more these days–my sins
catching up with me." When asked what sins those might be,
he kissed my hand. "By no means would I cloud that lovely face
with thought of my unsavory little adventures. How terribly gauche
that would make me." Then he stood up, told me that just conversing
with me had been a rest–that was his word, "conversing"–and mentioned
that he came by here each day. There were other talks. But the damage had
been done. Seduced? Not in the gold-toothed, diamond pinky ring, traveling
salesman way you mean. But all those flaws, those snags your imagination could
catch on, stories implied in everything he said or didn't say. What sins? How fallen?
Two to three, line, triangle. What stories did I have? What choice was there, once I understood?

Now the rains don't come, and the crops are ruined, or the river floods and drowns us out, blight, locusts, the bad son kills the good, the influenza epidemic of '03. And your grandfather hardly talks to me any more; I have no idea what he's thinking, except that he's bitter, and blames me. Well, let him. I started the story. Stories are about falling, about things getting old, complicated. Apples must to brandy in the cellars, disease raises the bread, blue threads grow to webs in the cheese–civilization depends on the harnessing of rot. You ride it as it pulls you down. Try telling him that, though.

Attic Shape

This room floats
over any stillness
or water drinking grey light.

Here it
hovers like a white paper
lantern, above the calm Atlantic.

The monastic walls are empty
of any other pictured thought;
the blind lifts, suggesting flight.

That kind of sagging fold-up bed the host pulls out
for the last guest he can accommodate, in the attic bedroom,
sheets bleached and worn to a purity

which completes silence.
No one will hear us, not the implied house
or the pale Atlantic

Keening spring, slap of blind, caught breath
suggesting flight, always
just now, just now

Enameled Crucifix

BODY   Birch white, bowed out
       Like the archer's yew.

ARMS   Stretched over
       The rack of the land,

HANDS   Nailed fast to the
       Hills from whence cometh
       Pollen yellow llamas with red heads, green feet.
       Under his singularly cheerful rose and turquoise

HALO   His

MOUTH   'S a slight bow, sardonic and sad and
       Wise as hills, as if

HIS BLOOD Made them green, and He were
       Glad of it.

FEET   Anchored to the neighborhood,
       In the Zen-empty circle of the village common His stick

LEGS   Make a Maypole for the dance of
       Jubilant chimneys and windows
       Open to joy, their lace drapes lifted up by light wind.

This cost twenty-three dollars. When my mother was given it by friends, she was overwhelmed with love. She hung it on the south wall, between two sheaves of dried dyed wheat.

Christ hung on the world, our painting in the grand
Allegorical manner–

HANDS   His hands our hills,

FEET   His feet our homes.

BLOOD   What element, earth-blood or ether, is not caught up in symbol
In the interstices of His crossed paradox?

ARMS   What is not encompassed by that backwards contorted,
Nailed down embrace?

The sea isn't shown, but we know it's there.
Most of the animals of El Salvador are present.
The damned get left out.

LEGS   The lavender dove flies down the cross's leg.

HALO   To bask in the halos of the gathered saints.

MOUTH   Ave Maria, their lips say, or maybe Ave Mort.
They could be saying
Anything. Breathless in this
Wind-lifted, dove-descending joy,
They stand glad unto nonsense.

BODY   Jesus too is winded, body white as cloth.
Not a bow but a sail, fixed to suffering's mast
Propelling us with infinite slowness

To a nation no less colorful
Or various in its beasts,
Not a new, but an edited earth.
The damned, the damned, the damned.

The Still Wet Mud Tablets of the Law I

IA

IB

א aleph/ox–one god
ב bet/house–no made image
ג gimel/camel–name in vain
ד dalet/door–Sabbath rest
ה hey/window–honor to parents
ו vav/hook–shall not kill
ז zayin/weapon–no adultery
ח chet/fence–shall not steal
ט tet/snake–no false witness
י yud/hand–not covet
(כ, kaf, 20, is palm of hand, 30 is ל/lamed/ox-goad,

(I want to fall down on my knees, it is so beautiful,
 the poem that I made.

God I'm tired, but then I've been working on
this for three days straight. "Be a computer analyst,"
my father says.   –Ugh! Cockroach!–
Got him. Think I'll go out with the people from next
door; they fight, but he's fun to look at. I need some
more material anyway. I'll show them my poem. He'll
say…and I'll say, "No, no, I'm not a genius, and I
don't want to be one,"
                 and so on.)

The Still Wet Mud Tablets of the Law II

These words:[1]

Egypt.[2]	–more than one history of the world
before*[3]	–*yesh. rak. echad.*
graven[4]	– < MGr. *eiconocklastes* < LGr. *eikon* (see ICON)
	+ *klaein,* to break: for IE. base see CALAMITY
oaths[5]	–remembered taste of soap
seventh[6]	–Adventist. And the *shabbas goy* opening the light
father, mother [7]	–a card for you, on your special day
murder[8]	–study exceptions
cleanliness	–I don't mind being ravished I just don't want to get muddy
thievery	–red handed, filthy handed
testimony[9]	–*Emet* was the motto of my university.
want[10]	–Susannah bathing, also
	–"Let's move to Pangea"–something else I wish I'd said

*Or *besides*

1	i.e "the ten words" originally each a short utterance
2	in Jewish tradition the first commandment
3	because *jealous*
4	rivers, wine were personified and statues of them worshiped
5	knowledge of the name = magical control
6	*holy* = separated
7	in Deuteronomy above the verse on parents the page heading reads *The law to be written upon stones. Curses.*
8	…electric chair…war…
9	This law demands…a suit involving a neighbor.
10	However, *neighbor's house* probably includes what is enumerated: wife, manservant, etc.

The Still Wet Mud Tablets of The Law III

God said I am the LORD that brought you out of bondage; you will worship no gods but Me. You
When he left, we felt like we had woken from a long sleep. What dream of virtue had held us? We

will remember this, or suffer to the third and fourth generation. Take My name in vain and I kill
couldn't remember. By three or four, the orgy was underway. That sweet bad wine singing in

you. I made the world in six days; you don't need a whole week for your pathetic jobs. Obey your
our throats, women's necklines getting lower and lower, and the make-up was put on with a

parents and I won't shorten your lives. Don't murder, have affairs, steal, lie in court, or lust after
trowel. People using new hundred-dollar bills to light their cigars and hookahs, betting on crapshoots,

your neighbor's house, wife, staff, ass, etc. There, that should do it. Now you'd better take these tablets
dancing the striptease (unwisely, in some cases). And the noise, the police were at the front, five

and go, no, you'd better get out of My way, because I am going to *kill* those little ingrates—
people had passed out on the floor, and I was sick all over Brad's shoes, for which he did not

thank me, *at* all.

l
el
yah
babelujah bablel ya alel
alleluh baalal ja Bab-ilu
allelujah Babylon babel
to us I reach I say my hand aloud allowed
mouth jawing at sounds, that God is, is, is near
To one next to me I say this, watch his foam cornered
we pierce heaven, and nothing we imagine will be kept from us.
at base of walls that tilt in, to teach the eye, thus, heart, this: we are a tower, a sword,
as the plains grow small. Mind, making, one leap, and the hod-carriers become ants
riches, their need for height was sore. Laid brick, and now are laying, grown tireless
for smooth face. Made the needle gate layer on layer, to thread the vault–living among
Then began to build, setting brick in bitumen: the rough for center, and the fine burnt
And they found slime for mortar, bitumen dug from earth, and inscribed and set the foundation stone.
into each the rounded tops to give the mortar purchase. They dried them in sun, or some they burnt.
erase ever. Then did they cut clay, then molded brick to be their stones, pushing thumb prints twice
in shouting distance, at least." They heaped up the earth, made height from flat, that water would not
They were one people, said with one voice, "Go to, let us build a mountain that is high enough to be
God would surely forget them, for on no high place could they build a temple and make supplication.
Nonetheless, they saw those plains would scatter them, and the rich earth drink their name like water.
Then they descended to the land of Shinar, and made their dwelling beside the river, in that plenty.

Ziggurat

/75

Muse as Library as Man in White Shirt

In bird cry of bronze
hinges, pulling to the brown-
and-gold paneled oak door. Sharp or cold
latch clicks hard, edge-lighting
dazzle off the dust-
fine snow

snapped out. Breath curls white, stamping off snow.
The library guide is waiting, bronze
eyes looking elsewhere, hair colorless as dust.
From the dim brown
of the vestibule he turns, birdlight
trick of joints, from cold

to cold
snow
light,
bronze
brown
dust.

Rich in dust,
the library, and cold,
a long high avenue of brown
leather and gilt flaking from bindings, snowing
leaf-like down. Shelves ending in busts of bronze
Greek philosophers, say, Victorian statesmen, or light-

-as-air bird skeletons in a glass case. Steep diagonals of sunlight,
birches in bright dust.
The guide is the angular and slightly bored bronze
soul of this grove. Hands under his arms, because it is cold.
I follow in and out of shadow the snowy
back of his shirt to a table in a shadow, a lit lamp, a brown and

ancient open book. I'd rather the shortcut, brown
study to take me in, connect me to the lit,
the molecular seeming of snow.
He sees what all I wish to know, the inner bark, the paths of dust;
his body would be ocean breathing in a shell, a pleasing cold.
Instead, I take my seat beneath the bronze

lamp's bronze light, bear-brown the long dusk. Sit in distraction (bright
snow), and hardly read the book, *Cold Dust,* that lies open there.

On the Beach

You might have encountered it this way: A knight and his squire have reached the eaves of the Dark Wood. The squire sits on his heels, watches the knight. The knight's face is set toward the trees, but he does not see them, or how the road vanishes into them so quickly. He sees his object, how golden it is. He seems, in fact, to have bent his thoughts on this end so completely that it dwells in him, and radiates from him, his luminous face, the eaves of forest.

Or this: A group of children saying "I dare you" to a girl at the side door of a house. Her friend would like to go in with her, is too frightened. Everyone knows about the ghosts there. The winter evening already dark. A car turns and passes; its headlights flash on the one unboarded window.

The man and woman have reached the border. From a hill on the other side, a mirror signal–"Safe now," "Come ahead." In the snow he will leave tracks, but the pines will give him cover. She doesn't love him enough to go with him. Also, a woman dreamed that she and her lover stood at the doors of an elevator, the green arrow lit and the bell sounded; when the doors opened she got on. He didn't. But sometimes the companion embarks on the journey also.

He or she, with the maid she loves as a sister, the devoted but slightly shorter friend. About to leave for or just returned from woods/ocean/underworld/sky, they stand under the electric shadow of battle, and the lightning is a sword, or the sword flashes like lightning, or the setting or rising sun makes a brief red lamp below the day's clouds. However, when the moon was rising at the edge of the swamp, her hood fell back, and she was by her own light reflected in the foul water. She was herself hero, light, attendant, and edge of time, and static, for the branches caught her and she couldn't get free.

He stood at the mouth of the cave, felt its tomb-breath on his face. His friend was a horse too broken to protest. Nothing shone, but then, he wouldn't be coming back.

Monroe Street Harbor II

The blue the clouds
Fill and hide
Manifests itself, a film
(Thinly shining as gold leaf,

Viscous as an essential oil)
That surfaces the water.
Planar, and still
Irradiate from depths.

Depths harbored in the surfaces of things. These things.
Floats and vessels. Break wall embracing
A various array, a safety.

Cymbals crashing after long quiet
Help us to doubt our conservation.
Pierce us with the end point
Of the cornucopia, where the void becomes riches.
Let our own sons not know us; let us find our wives

Surrounded by lovers.
Make our homes startle us as
After years of war and voyage,
The terrible common day and its ending.

The strangeness of creation hurts me, first nothing, then something,
A flock of gulls scattering up
Into the landscape, a fractured simple voice.
Why from water and vapor to harbor, boat?
And once made, why

Continuing, now made, now made again
Like the crests of waves not breaking?
This concrete, this benchwood that bites
The leg–borning tensed in place, electric, unstable.

The eastern lake breathes out a little darkness
Without as yet tarnishing itself.
Southeast, the mills rise half out of water,
A darker, fainter exhalation,

Threaded by the breath of breath.
Whether made from nothing, or the fishy muck of chaos,
Their forms come from nothing, and the glamour
Of nothing is their halo.

What to Do with Inanimate Objects

Be infantile Take them
In your mouth

Go at them gum and tongue
Saliva, risk

And beach stones will break
Sweetly open like grapes

Buckshot will unfold itself
In the manner of

Chinese paper flowers then trail
From your mouth when you speak Hills also

Can be suckled into leaking
Lava or milk

Oh Sticky Chin

And that dry branch would love to go off
In a rapture of salt

Two Tourists with Guidebook Approach Planetarium

Eva Noodle: The wind! My hair
                            Is starting to grow sideways. What's this?

Eva Pick: The desired object, 900 Achsah Bond.

Noodle: It isn't really black.

Pick: Yet black is the effect.

Noodle: Beautifully polished.

Pick: Yes. Silver
                            Is really the effect.

Noodle: How many sides does it have? Of what
                            Material? And by what water?

Pick: By the Sea of Michigan salted
                            With mill waste, it is carved in rainbow granite,
                            But what metal domes the whole, the book doesn't say.
                            It has one side for each
                            House of heaven.

Noodle: And how
                            Are the houses connected?

Pick: By the grooved ghosts of columns at each corner,
            And above them the tenons
            Of square synechdochic coins, depicting
            Taurus' horn, Aries'
            Hoof, Virgo's hymen. They're Italian.

Noodle: What about enter and exit, window and door?

Pick: From here there are no windows,
            And the beveled doors would welcome only
            Splayed colors from the broken sun.
            Sinisterly intact, no one in or out, like an egg,

But actually people descend
            A glass cage by the sundial,
            And corrupt it from beneath.

Noodle: What a relief.
            Is it male?

Pick: It is far too
            Perfect to say. Curved,
            Geometrical, monumental
            Yet vague, not phallus or breast.

Noodle: Can it be translated?

Pick: Accurately. It says here, *Yesh*
La ets ha-chayim keter, or
De acerina reina o rey.

Noodle: With what paean does it inspire you?

Pick: The same as yours, thus;

> *O wave cohesive in quicksilver sea,*
> *Flagged with flowers of Venus foam;*
> *O their in ovum fortress child,*
> *Hematite hermaphrodite*
> *Leadenly nested in*
> *Dodecagonal splendor–*

Noodle: Enough. Still,
I don't feel I know it.

Pick: Start with the stones' red and black
Gneissosity, undulant flows of hornblende and quartz,
So that each side is the story
Of fluid galaxies, or maybe cell nuclei, emerging from some
Primal migraine.

And you can see the gulls are compelled
To stand at its base, all looking north
Where the wind comes from. When they occasionally
Rise and hang a few feet in air,
Spanning that push without motion

Except to open and close gold mouths,
That gives you context.

Noodle: Yes, and yet…
Why this stasis, when the sky dragons are
Blue-black and boiling?

Why does a gull sometimes keep rising,
Then veer off sideways and scream?
The flags are all at attention–what's going to happen?

Pick: Something more than the first fat hits
Of rain, than the guidebook resolving to fugitive leaves.

Noodle: Will the egg's cobalt casing break in the tension?
Will the comets spill out, the connected dots
Of constellations? Will our mapped stars fly up,
Overlaying the real ones resonantly like
Notes on a glass harmonica, and other times
Tangling and impeding their orbits?

Pick: Or I will.

Notes and Sources

Page 5: *Hermes as a Victim of His Own Nature;* John Dee referred in his writings to the all "contained in the ovular form of the alchemist's egg," as paraphrased by Peter French in his *John Dee: The World of an Elizabethan Magus.*

Page 14: *Waiting Table; benami* is an Arabic legal term meaning "in absentia;" the Sarabaites were a medieval order of monks that forswore having permanent homes.

Page 30: *Nothing Framed Is Absent;* the italicized passage is from a letter written by Columbus proposing his journey to Japan and the Spice Islands.

Page 34: *"Can't See Fuji/—Interesting;"* the title is quoted from haiku of Basho's; it appears in Robert Hass's *Essential Haiku.* There is a series of stations where climbers can eat and spend the night along the trail that goes up Mount Fuji.

Page 37: *fude:* writing brush.

Page 38: *Endnotes;* sources for this poem include W. G. Aston's translation of the *Nihongi,* William de Bary's *Sources of Japanese Tradition,* William Boorstin's *Discoverers,* Donald Keene's *Anthology of Japanese Literature,* James L. Larson's *Reason and Experience: The Representation of Natural Order in the Work of Carl von Linne,* Jisaburo Ohwi's *Flora of Japan,* Donald L. Philippi's translation of the *Kojiki,* William C. H. Robert's wonderfully literal translation of *Coen's Voyage to Cathay, Tartary and the Islands East of Japan, 1643,* and Post Wheeler's *The Sacred Scriptures of the Japanese.*

Page 58: Dictated by a fellow passenger on the Jeffrey Express.

Page 73: *The Still Wet Mud Tablets of the Law II; There is more than one history of the world* is one of the reiterated themes of John Crowley's *Ægypt.* The notes are emended from the *New Oxford Annotated Bible.*

Page 78: *On the Beach;* I am indebted to Professor Alexandra Olsen of the University of Denver for the knowledge of the dramatic convention in Germanic poetry here illustrated.

Page 82: *Two Tourists with Guidebook Approach Planetarium;* the structure being described is the Adler Planetarium in Chicago.

Page 84: The Hebrew means "There is to the tree of life a crown;" the Spanish, "Of hematite queen or king."